# ANCIENT EGYPT

# Tutankhamun

The brief reign of the boy-king Tutankhamun was of little significance in the grand sweep of Egyptian history. But it was the remains of this obscure king, long-hidden in a treasure-filled tomb, which outlasted the ravages of time and tomb robbers. In 1922 Howard Carter's stunning archaeological find created a phenomenal increase in the public's awareness of ancient Egypt and its fascination with Tutankhamun.

## Contents

*The DVD symbol, which appears throughout the book, highlights points of specific interest in the film.*

1

# Who was Tutankhamun?

Tutankhamun, the boy-king, was the son of Akhenaten, a long-serving Egyptian king. Pharaoh of all Egypt, Tutankhamun was on the throne for less than a decade and was dead by the age of nineteen, but his tomb became an exciting archaeological find.

## Family life

Historians believe Tutankhamun was not the son of Akhenaten's first wife, Queen Nefertiti, but of another wife, Queen Kiya. He was known as Tutankhaten and came to the throne in 1333 BC at the age of nine or ten. He was crowned at Memphis and married Ankhesenamun, a half-sister who was slightly older than him.

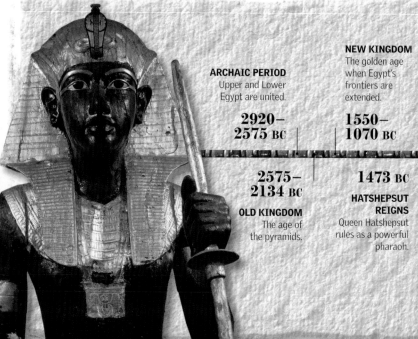

**ARCHAIC PERIOD**
Upper and Lower Egypt are united.

**2920– 2575 BC**

**NEW KINGDOM**
The golden age when Egypt's frontiers are extended.

**1550– 1070 BC**

**2575– 2134 BC**

**OLD KINGDOM**
The age of the pyramids.

**1473 BC**

**HATSHEPSUT REIGNS**
Queen Hatshepsut rules as a powerful pharaoh.

**THE KING'S FATHER**
Akhenaten, shown here with his first wife Nefertiti, was the father of Tutankhamun.

## Troubled times

The boy-king's reign was during the Amarna period, a time of religious instability when worship of the Sun-god Aten, associated with his father, Akhenaten, was still practiced. Akhenaten had ruled from Amarna, a new capital of Egypt on the east bank of the Nile, instead of from the old religious capital of Luxor (Thebes). Akhenaten's insistence on worshipping the Sun-god Aten, to the exclusion of all other gods, caused deep divisions within the community. Although he was born in Amarna, the boy-king later moved back to the old capital, Luxor. He was young and vulnerable. Probably on the advice of Ay, his father's main vizier (adviser) and Horemheb, the commander of the army, he changed his name to Tutankhamun and reinstated worship of the previously dominant god, Amun.

**EGYPTOLOGY**
Lord Carnavon visits Egypt and acquires a taste for archaeology.

**KING TUTANKHAMUN**
Tutankhamun ascends to the Egyptian throne.

**1333–1323 BC**

**1903**

**TOMB OPENED**
Carter discovers the Tomb of Tutankhamun

**1922**

**1290–1224 BC**

Rameses II is on the throne for 65 years.

**RAMESES II REIGNS**

**332 BC**

**EMPIRE OF ALEXANDER**
The Greek ruler Alexander the Great delivers Egypt from harsh Persian rulers.

**1907–1914**

**EXCAVATIONS**
Howard Carter works at Lord Carnarvon's excavations at Luxor and Aswan.

# How Did He Die?

For a long time it was thought Tutankhamun's sudden death at the age of 19 was murder. As with any detective story, historians have examined the records for who might have committed murder and who benefited from the king's death. Excitingly, modern technology has contributed some new clues.

## In the frame

In early examinations of Tutankhamun's mummy it appeared that he might have died from injuries, which led to theories as to why he might have been killed. As the young king was just old enough to start making his own decisions, suspicion fell on his royal advisers, Ay and Horemheb. After his death, Ay ruled as pharaoh for four years and may have married Tutankhamun's widow Ankhesenamun.

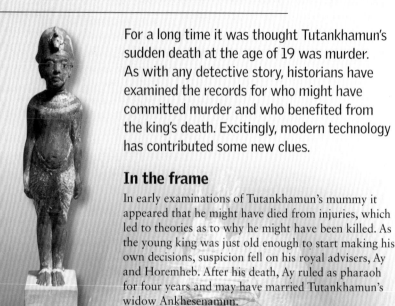

**THE VICTIM**
Historians are still debating whether the premature death of the young king was from natural causes.

**FATAL INJURY?**
The king's death may have resulted from an accident. Medical treatment at the time was limited to herbal preparations and balms. In the ancient world serious infections, such as gangrene, could kill within just a few days.

## Injuries sustained

Could Tutankhamun have died from a head wound? A hole was found at the base of his skull, but rather than an injury, scientists now believe the aperture was made during the preparation of his body for burial, a process that involved injecting a resin into the skull to preserve it. It was also discovered that Tutankhamun's body had a broken thighbone, perhaps from an accident prior to his death.

## Open verdict

By examining CT (computed tomography) scans of the thigh injury, scientists now suggest the severe break may have resulted from a riding accident and that the king could have died of an infection arising from such a serious trauma. The latest evidence supports the theory that Tutankhamun died as a result of accidental injury, but is not conclusive. We may never be absolutely sure whether his death was murder or misadventure.

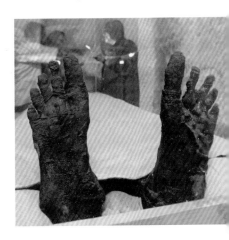

## WHAT DID TUTANKHAMUN REALLY LOOK LIKE?

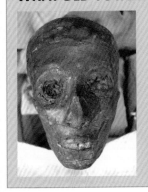

In 2005 a new CT scanning process produced around 17,000 images of Tutankhamun's head and body. Scientists from the Cairo Museum, Cairo University and observation teams from Italy and Switzerland used the scans to reconstruct the face of the boy-king. It is that of a serious, good-looking young man with smooth, clear skin, even features and slightly bucked teeth. The golden death mask recognized throughout the world as one of the most iconic images of Egypt can be regarded as a good likeness of the youthful Tutankhamun.

# The Greatest Find

Excavation of the royal burial grounds in the Valley of the Kings was conducted over many years. An American archaeologist, Theodore Davis, first held the permit. Later it was held by the English archaeologist Howard Carter, working for his patron, an English peer, the Earl of Carnarvon. All had dreamed of locating the elusive tomb of Tutankhamun.

**THE TOMB ENTRANCE**
Lord Carnarvon, his daughter, Evelyn Herbert, and Howard Carter at the tomb entrance that was buried beneath the entrance to the tomb of Rameses VI.

## 'Wonderful things!'

Carter identified the seals on the doorway as those of King Tutankhamun. Inside, Carter and Carnarvon descended a sloping passage. Carter made a hole in a second door and lit a candle to test for dangerous gases. He peered through the hole with a torch. 'Can you see anything?' asked Carnarvon. 'Yes' came the reply, 'I can see wonderful things!' Carter picked out the shapes of statues, animal figures and furniture, all glinting with gold.

## Patience rewarded

Howard Carter searched for Tutankhamun's tomb for almost ten years and had experienced many disappointments. In early 1922, after months of working alone, Carter pleaded with Carnarvon to fund a final year's digging. In November his workmen uncovered a sunken flight of steps. Carnarvon joined Carter and together they breached a doorway covered in ancient plaster.

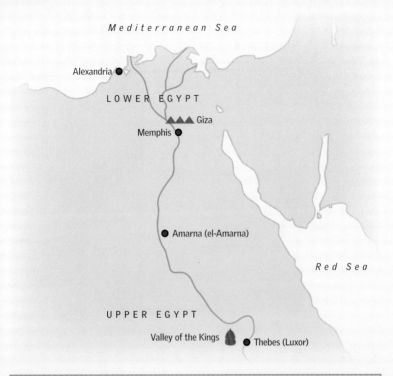

Mediterranean Sea

Alexandria ●

LOWER EGYPT

▲▲▲ Giza
Memphis ●

Amarna (el-Amarna) ●

Red Sea

UPPER EGYPT

Valley of the Kings
Thebes (Luxor) ●

# HOWARD CARTER AND LORD CARNARVON

The Earl of Carnarvon was a sports enthusiast who only developed an interest in archaeology after a motoring accident left him very weak. Carnarvon's doctor advised him to escape a cold, damp English winter, so he traveled to Egypt. There he took an interest in 'Egyptology.' After several weeks digging near Luxor he unearthed only a mummified cat, complete with a small wooden coffin, but this was enough to spark a strong interest in organizing further excavations. To help him, he hired Howard Carter, an Englishman who had worked for the Egyptian Antiquities Service under the distinguished French Egyptologist Gaston Maspero. Together, Carter and Carnarvon would make the most remarkable archaeological find in modern times, the tomb of Tutankhamun.

# A Simple Tomb

The tomb of Tutankhamun is one of the smallest in the Valley of the Kings. The pharaohs used the valley, after abandoning the pyramids of Lower Egypt, in the hope the tombs would be safe from grave robbers. Tutankhamun's tomb was one of the few that survived virtually intact.

## Secret and silent

The isolated Valley of the Kings near Luxor was a complex burial site with many hidden entrances and false tombs. It was designed to confuse and deter tomb robbers attracted by the vast wealth that was buried with the dead. The stone is good quality white limestone and the steep-sided valley offered great expanse to excavate intricate tombs. The ingenuity of the masons and workmen in sealing the rooms of the tomb with plaster also kept many tombs hidden. It is not surprising that the area acquired a reputation as the most mysterious and exciting of all Egyptian excavation sites.

**VALLEY OF THE KINGS**
The Valley of the Kings is a wadi, a dry watercourse, in a barren desert. From the 16th to 11th centuries BC, Egyptian pharaohs built their tombs there. The entrances to the tombs of Tutankhamun and Rameses VI are shown here.

**A QUICK BURIAL**
Tutankhamun's burial was relatively simple by a pharaoh's standards. His tomb had only four main rooms, made ready quickly due to his unexpected death. In contrast, tombs of older pharaohs were prepared over decades and consisted of many rooms.

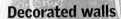

## Decorated walls

The murals in Tutankhamun's tomb are simple compared to other major Egyptian tombs and appear to have been painted in haste. The images inside the burial chamber include hieroglyphs of Tutankhamun's name and scenes depicting the young king in life, and also following his death in the after-life. In one scene Tutankhamun is met by Nut, goddess of the sky, and mother of all goddesses. In another he is welcomed to the underworld by Osiris, the king of the dead.

## AN INSIDE JOB?

Despite the many precautions the tomb builders took, tomb security was a constant problem. False entrances were built into the design of many tombs, as well as special seals and empty chambers, all aimed at deflecting would-be robbers. In addition, necropolis guards were deployed, and guardian statues and magic talismans were left to protect against intruders. Construction teams were quartered in special camps and their numbers kept to a minimum in order to prevent knowledge of the whereabouts of tombs becoming widespread. But many tombs were robbed soon after they were sealed – sometimes within hours of completion.

# Boxes within Boxes

## Watch It

**An image from the side** of a decorated chest depicts Tutankhamun on a golden chariot. He was an avid sportsman and was in training to be a soldier. The tomb held many items of sporting and military equipment.

Even after reaching the main entrance off the tomb it was another three months before Howard Carter was able to locate the Holy Grail of his excavation, Tutankhamun's sarcophagus. Only after clearing the antechamber and annex was he able to explore the burial chamber itself and reveal the most exciting secrets of the pharaoh's tomb.

**WAKING THE PHARAOH**
Howard Carter, A.R. Callahan and an Egyptian foreman look through the doors of the four gilded shrines to the sarcophagus at the tomb of Tutankhamun.

## Golden sarcophagus

Within four gilded and inlaid, heavy wooden shrines, Carter discovered a richly decorated sarcophagus of golden-yellow quartz covered by a pink granite lid that was painted to match the base. Inside was a nest of three heavy coffins, the innermost made of solid gold. All fitted together so tightly that an improvised crane was needed to lift them out.

**THE KING'S MASK**
The burnished gold of the mask is of the highest quality, and the inlays of blue faience, semi-precious metals and blue lapis lazuli are all the result of a fine attention to detail.

## The eyes have it

Inside the last coffin lay Tutankhamun's mummy, tightly wrapped in a linen shroud and protected by an array of more than 100 precious jewels and charms. The finest of all the treasures, however, was the fabulous death mask sculpted from beaten gold. The mask's image is of the boy-king's young face, made up as Osiris, King of the Dead, with striped headcloth, pigtail and beard. The craftsmanship of the mask is exquisite. The eyes, made of yellow quartz with black obsidian for the pupils, give the mask an eerily life-like gaze that still has the power to engage all who see it.

## THE EMBALMERS' CRAFT

To preserve the dead, Egyptian priests removed the internal organs, including the heart, liver, lungs and intestines – the brain was usually removed via the nose and the skull filled with a preservative resin. Organs were preserved separately in special vessels called canopic jars. The body was washed and rubbed with salt to remove all moisture, then left to dry for about a month. It was then rubbed with oils and perfumes, before being packed with sawdust, mud or sand and wrapped tightly in resin-soaked bandages.

**THE ART OF EMBALMING**
This alabaster box seated upon a gilded wooden sled once held the viscera of Tutankhamun.

# 'Wonderful Things'

When Carter first sighted the objects he described as 'wonderful things' he did not yet know the full extent of the treasure trove within the tomb. It was packed with an extraordinary collection of objects intended to accompany Tutankhamun on his journey to the afterlife.

## Journey to the kingdom of Osiris

The ancient Egyptians believed that after death, people traveled to the land of Osiris, the kingdom of the dead. To help them make this journey they were buried with many of their possessions, together with food and clothes that they enjoyed during their lifetime. As the weeks passed Carter and his assistants uncovered an astonishing range of furniture, pottery, weaponry and models, including boats for travel in the hereafter.

**WEAPONS**
Daggers (left), throwing sticks, clubs, boomerangs and bows and arrows were for the deceased to defend himself on the journey to the kingdom of the dead.

## Eternal life

The gods were required to help with the deceased's journey to the after-life and more than fifty statues of deities were found in the tomb. These guardian statues included a figure of the 'jackal' god, Anubis, and a gilded cow's head of the goddess Hathor, the goddess of fertility and the fields.

**SHABTI**
The figurines known as 'shabtis' were intended to act as servants to the deceased in the afterlife.

## For the afterlife

As well as guardian statues, the tomb contained more than 400 wooden figurines, complete with headdresses, which are known as 'shabtis.' Along with the finely carved figurines were almost 2,000 miniature tools and agricultural implements such as yokes, hoes and picks, providing a fascinating window on Egyptian daily life and farming practices at the time of Tutankhamun.

**FACTFILE**

**Perfume and cosmetics**
Alabaster perfume vessels (below) and many cosmetic items were in the tomb. Perfume and cosmetics interested the ancient Egyptians, who were skillful chemists and inventors. The Egyptians took care of their appearance; they used cosmetics and ointments and dyed their hair with henna.

### Watch It

**The elaborate golden throne** of King Tutankhamun (left) was described by Lord Carnarvon as 'one of the most marvelous pieces of furniture that has ever been discovered.' The panel on the back of the chair is richly inlaid and shows the king and his wife, Ankhesenamun, inside an elaborate pavilion that is open to the powerful, life-enhancing rays of the sun.

# Time Capsule

Practical and decorative items of all kinds were found in Tutankhamun's tomb – from tools and lamps, stone and metal pots and vessels, to fans, baskets and games. Among the most highly prized items are the boxes, gold and jewelery.

**TREASURE TROVE**
Carter and Carnarvon found grave goods of extraordinary quality totaling more than 5,000 items. It was a time capsule the likes of which had never been discovered before.

## Boxes and chests

The decorated boxes are among the finest examples of craftsmanship found in Tutankhamun's tomb. The Painted Box was thought by Carter to be one of the most sublime objects. The entire surface of the box is covered with beautifully executed illustrations of the king's life, mainly depicting him in action scenes. In one he rides on a chariot against the Syrian foe, his mouth turned down in a serious expression of concentration as he prepares to fire an arrow. The image is of a brave and fearless king – or a king in the making. In another scene, Tutankhamun takes part in a lion hunt while riding on his chariot.

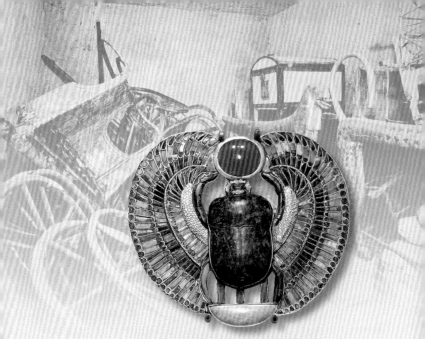

## Beads, bangles and bracelets

The jewelery found in the tomb ranged from the simplest glass beads, pendants, bracelets and earrings to necklaces of great beauty incorporating intricate patterns and requiring exacting craftsmanship. One gold necklace is formed by a scarab (beetle) holding a solar disc within a complex pattern of glass and semi-precious stones.

**BOUNTY OF EGYPT**
The tomb included gilded figures, chariots, thrones, couches, jewelery and many other precious artifacts, as well as fans, baskets and games.

## HISTORIC FOOTPRINTS

It is only a stroke of luck that Tutankhamun's tomb was not robbed of its treasures in ancient times. When Carter first examined the interior of the tomb he realized that thieves had broken into the antechamber in ancient times but must have been disturbed by the necropolis guards and fled. Objects were strewn around in disarray, no doubt returned in haste by the guards as best they could. Remarkably, when Carter had first entered the antechamber he saw that the footprints of the thieves were still clearly visible in the dust on the floor.

# Riches from the Land

**Beautiful blue**
Egyptian blue faience is a
very hard material usually
made from a combination
of ground quartz and potash
(potassium oxide) or natron,
in a self-glazing paste. In
ancient times faience was
used with earthenware, tin,
bronze and other metals and
was widely used for decorating
vessels and jewelery. Faience
was used for parts of
Tutankhamun's death mask,
including the vulture on his
forehead, which together
with the cobra next to it was
designed to protect the king
in the afterlife. Blue was a
favorite color as it was thought
to 'glisten with a light symbolic
of life, rebirth and immortality.'

The golden treasures taken from
the tomb of Tutankhamun are
testimony to both the labor of
miners in ancient times and to the
skill of craftsman who fashioned
the metal into gleaming grave
goods. But where did all this gold,
and the dazzling array of precious
stones, come from? The gold
found in Tutankhamun's tomb
came either from the deserts of
eastern Egypt, or from the rich
mines of Nubia, to the south, the
very name of which meant 'gold.'

**GOLDEN SUNSHADE**
A gold ceremonial sunshade, inlaid with turquoise,
lapis-lazuli and carnelian, shows the king's
'cartouche,' a group of hieroglyphic symbols.

## Mineral wealth

The great wealth of Egypt was based on minerals, the fertile agricultural plain of the River Nile and trade with other countries of the eastern Mediterranean. By Tutankhamun's time, in the 14th century BC, the silver and gold of the Upper Nile had been exploited for centuries, along with precious and semi-precious stones such as obsidian, deep blue lapis-lazuli, carnelian from the eastern desert and turquoise from the Sinai. All were prized for their decorative appeal.

### DID YOU KNOW?

**Flesh of the gods**
One of ancient Egypt's most important gods, Amun-Ra, was known as the Sun-God. Because the shiny surface of polished gold was thought to resemble sunlight, gold was regarded as the very 'flesh of the gods.'

## Going for gold

Conditions in the Nubian gold mines were appalling. The mines, in remote and waterless locations, were often worked only in the cooler months. The miners were probably slaves – prisoners of war and convicted criminals. At Wadi Hammamat, the most northerly of the eastern desert mines, veins of the precious metal were encased in quartz and could only be extracted by crushing rock, which required a great deal of manpower. Miners had to carry loosened chunks of ore to the surface for processing.

**GOLD MINERS**
This map is of the gold mines of King Wadi Hammamat. A contemporary account describes mine workers 'in the dark in these winding tunnels, they carry torches that are affixed to their foreheads.'

# The Fascination Endures

Since Howard Carter's discovery of Tutankhamun's tomb in 1922, the sheer exoticism of the boy-king who ruled briefly at the zenith of Egyptian civilization has not left the public imagination. Hundreds of exhibitions have been held since the tomb's discovery and attendances continue to grow. In the 1920s 'Tutmania' spawned a branch of Art Deco design in architecture and film, with jewelery designs featuring Egyptian icons.

**TUTMANIA**
Building like this historic theatre in Atlanta, Georgia, were inspired by the discovery of Tutankhamun's tomb and other Egyptian treasures. This 1920s neo-Egyptian Art-Deco style was popular in many countries. Jewelery designs also featured Egyptian icons, such as sphinxes, hieroglyphics, pyramids, masks and headdresses.

## Tutmania in the 1920s

Enthusiasts for the pharaoh nicknamed 'King Tut' included movie directors and architects. They discovered Egyptian-inspired designs at the Paris Exhibition of the Decorative Arts in 1925. Inspired partly by ancient Egypt, the Art Deco movement took off in Europe, the US and around the world, influencing cinema design, civic buildings, factories and transport hubs. Interior design in lighting and fabrics, fashion, cigarette cases and picture frames all drew inspiration from 'Egyptienerie,' the artifacts of ancient Egypt.

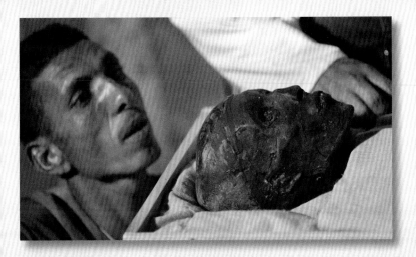

**PUBLIC EXPOSURE**
The true face of
Tutankhamun was
revealed to the public
recently. His mummy was
moved from its ornate
sarcophagus to a nearby
climate-controlled case
where experts say it will
be better preserved.

## Meet King Tut

The main items of the Tutankhamun collection
in the Egyptian Museum, Cairo, are among the
most popular exhibits, but until recently only
50 people had ever seen the real face of King
Tutankhamun. Now millions will be able to
see him. In November 2007 Tutankhamun's
mummy was moved to new surroundings within
the Cairo Museum. His mummy now lives in
a climate-controlled, air-conditioned gallery
in order to preserve it, especially his face – the
most valuable part.

## A MUMMY'S CURSE: LORD CARNARVON DIES

Superstition and legend swirled around the
discovery of the tomb. Lord Carnarvon died
unexpectedly from an infected mosquito bite
within a year of the discovery of Tutankhamun's
mummy. Only two weeks earlier, novelist Marie
Corelli had asserted in an article that anyone
entering a sealed tomb would meet with 'dire
punishment.' Strangely, the lights of Cairo went
out at exactly the time of Carnarvon's death.

# Test Your Knowledge

**1** What was Tutankhamun's name before he changed it?
 a) Akhenaten
 b) Tutanhkaten
 c) Amenhotep III

**2** Which queen is thought to have been Tutankhamun's mother?
 a) Nefertiti
 b) Kiya
 c) Hatshepsut

**3** Who was the wife of Tutankhamun?
 a) Nefertiti
 b) Ankhesenamun
 c) Cleopatra

**4** What is the name of the period during which Tutankhamun lived?
 a) The Amarna period
 b) The 18th Dynasty
 c) The New Kingdom

**5** Where was Tutankhamun crowned Pharaoh?
 a) Thebes
 b) Memphis
 c) Valley of the Kings

*A secondary wife of Akhenaten, and possibly the mother of Tutankamun, who is depicted on this canopic jar?*

How much have you learned about Tutankhamun from this book and the DVD?

*Archaeologist Howard Carter and colleague examine Tutankhamun's coffin.*

**6** **When did Tutankhamun come to the throne?**
a) 2333 BC
b) 1933 BC
c) 1333 BC

**7** **About how long was the reign of Tutankhamun?**
a) 20 years
b) 30 years
c) 10 years

**8** **What is a vizier?**
a) A scribe
b) An adviser
c) A priest

**9** **In which year did Howard Carter discover the entrance to Tutankhamun's tomb?**
a) 1912
b) 1920
c) 1922

**10** **Below which tomb did Howard Carter find the entrance to Tutankhamun's tomb?**
a) Akhenhaten
b) Thutmose III
c) Rameses VI

**13** Which French Egyptologist worked for the Egyptian Antiquities Service at the time of Carter's discovery?
a) François Champollion
b) Gaston Maspero
c) André Citröen

*The mask of Tutankhamun is one of the most iconic images of ancient Egypt.*

**14** Which semi-precious stone was used to make the pupils of Tutankhamun's eyes in the death mask?
a) Quartz
b) Amethyst
c) Obsidian

**11** Who sponsored Howard Carter's excavations in the Valley of the Kings?
a) Gaston Maspero
b) Theodore Davis
c) Lord Carnarvon

**15** What color is lapis-lazuli?
a) Red
b) Black
c) Blue

**12** What do experts believe to be a likely cause of Tutankhamun's death?
a) A blow to the head
b) An infection after a broken leg
c) Old age

**16** A likeness of the head of which creature was next to the cobra on the forehead of Tutankhamun's death mask?
a) A dog
b) A hippopotamus
c) A vulture

**17** In legend, the god Osiris ruled which kingdom?
a) The Kingdom of the Upper Nile
b) The Kingdom of the Dead
c) The Kingdom of Heliopolis

**18** How many coffins were inside the Sarcophagus?
a) 30
b) 3
c) 13

**19** Where were the internal organs of the dead stored?
a) Guardian statues
b) Canopic jars
c) Wooden chests

**20** In what year did the Paris Exhibition of the Decorative Arts feature Egyptian designs?
a) 1919
b) 1920
c) 1925

*Which kingdom did the ancient Egyptians believe was ruled by the god they called Osiris?*

*Answers on page 24*

# Test Your Knowledge Answers

1(b)  The name means 'living image of the god Aten.'
2(b)  Kiya may have died shortly after giving birth.
3(b)  She was his half-sister.
4(a)  Amarna was the name of a new capital.
5(b)  Memphis was an older capital.
6(c)  He was only nine or ten years old.
7(c)  He was dead by the age of 19.
8(b)  Tutankhamun's main adviser was Ay.
9(c)  He worked in Egypt most of his life.
10(c)  The entrance had been covered since 1148.

11(c)  He was an English peer.
12(b)  Gangrene was a common infection.
13(b)  He was twice appointed head of the service.
14(c)  The whites were of yellow quartz.
15(c)  Blue symbolized life, rebirth and immortality.
16(c)  The vulture and the cobra were symbolic.
17(b)  He was depicted with a crown of reeds.
18(b)  The gold coffin weighed 220 pounds.
19(b)  Priests removed the internal organs.
20(c)  It sparked off Egyptian-inspired designs.

# Amazing Facts

• Howard Carter not only found the tomb of Tutankhamun but he was also responsible for locating the tombs of Queen Hatshepsut and King Tuthmose IV, the 'great grandfather' of Tutankhamun.

• Grave robbers failed to find Tutankhamun's tomb over many centuries. What kept it safe? The fact is the entrance had been buried by sand and rock in ancient times while other projects were carried out. Worker's huts were erected on top of the rubble for building the tomb of Rameses VI.

• Following his discovery of Tutankhamun's tomb with Lord Carnarvon, and after another ten years of painstaking cataloging of the artifacts,

Howard Carter retired from archaeological fieldwork. He lived a life of quiet seclusion after all the excitement of Tutankhamun. Eventually he returned to London, and in 1939 Carter died peacefully at the age of 65.

## Useful Websites

www.egyptianmuseum.gov.
eg/collection_tut.html
The official website of the Egyptian Museum has a special section devoted to Tutankhamun and offers a search facility to the extensive collection of artifacts.

www.metmuseum.org/explore/
newegypt/htm/a_index.htm
The Metropolitan Museum of Art in New York City houses a rich collection of Egyptian art, much of it collected by Theodore Davis. The website is a valuable online resource.

www.fieldmuseum.org/eternalegypt/
afterlife2.html
This website was developed in 2003 for a special exhibition at the Field Museum in Chicago, Illinois. Divided into seven themes, it has useful notes on the exhibits.